MMA DICTIONARY

Title: MMA Dictionary

I0156926

ISBN-13: 978-1-94282.

Desc: MMA Dictionary is an A-Z of key terms used in Mixed Martial Arts.

Author: Kambiz Mostofizadeh

Publisher: Mikazuki Publishing House

MMA DICTIONARY

Introduction

Martial Arts from various nations share similar techniques and have different names. All martial arts come from a similar source and that source is the human need to survive. Certain nations or peoples changed or adapted techniques from nations like Japan. It is easy to follow the movement of martial arts from nations within Asia to Western nations. Some martial arts are not easy traceable because they are indigenous to the peoples that practice them. Dumog is a perfect example of such a style. Martial artists train to be able to defend themselves and certain techniques overlap in several nations. A punch is a technique that is prevalent in several styles, from Kung Fu to

MMA DICTIONARY

Boxing to Karate to Tae Kwan Do. Who invented punching? Who invented the front kick? Who invented blocking? It seems that all cultures share a few similar techniques. Mixed Martial Arts has existed in various forms for over 2000 years. Mixed Martial Arts as a professional fighting combat sport has existed for less than fifty years. This book is not the "end all" of Mixed Martial Arts terminology, but rather it is a beginning point of reference to learn from. There will be new editions of this book released. Future editions will be updated with new terminology as needed.

MMA DICTIONARY

A

Abu Dhabi Combat Club – Famous grappling tournament hosted in Abu Dhabi in the United Arab Emirates. The greatest grapplers in the world compete for prestige and prizes.

Aiki – Harmonizing with the energy of your opponent in order to control it.

MMA DICTIONARY

Aikido – Martial Art created by Morehei Ueshiba that emphasizes on re-direction and yielding. Aikido was influenced by Kendo as well as Jujitsu, and it is observable in the movements of Aikido practitioners. Steven Seagal is famous for having promoted Aikido to Western nations.

Ali, Muhammad – World famous Heavyweight Boxing champion that became famous for his antics inside and outside of the ring. Influenced future generations of Boxing and MMA fighters. Muhammad Ali fought an MMA match, billed as an exhibition, against Japanese wrestler Antonio Inoki in Japan. The fight against Inoki lasted hours without any winner and resulted in Ali ending

MMA DICTIONARY

up in a hospital for injuries received during the bout.

Americana – Figure four armlock used by BJJ practitioners on the ground. The Americana creates a tight grip causing the opponent to feel trapped.

Anaconda Choke – A BJJ grappling submission technique similar to a triangle choke, except that the attacker's arms are used to apply the choke.

Arm Bar – Judo and Jujitsu technique known as Juji Gatame in Japanese. The Arm Bar technique became famous in Mixed Martial Arts matches, bringing this technique in to mainstream martial arts.

MMA DICTIONARY

Atemi – Punching techniques that focus on striking vital parts. Atemi is used to disrupt the attention of the opponent in order to create an opportunity for applying grappling techniques. Atemi is most used by Aikido practitioners as a means to create locking opportunities. Ninja used sand as Atemi while Aikido practitioners may use a simple punching technique as Atemi.

Arigato – Thank you in the Japanese language.

Ashi – Foot in the Japanese language.

Askren, Ben – Bellator MMA Welterweight Champion. Award winning Collegiate Wrestler.

MMA DICTIONARY

Axe Kick – Kick that is delivered like an axe with the heel being brought down on the opponent. Favored technique of Kyokushin Karate fighter Andy Hug.

Azuma, Takashi – Founder of Kudo Daido Juku, a Japanese mixed martial art that uses gloves and safety headgear in Kudo Daido Juku competitions. Before Kudo, Azuma created a style that incorporated Judo and Kyokushin Karate. Azuma holds a 9th Dan Black Belt in Kyokushin Karate. *See Kudo.*

B

Ba Gua – Chinese eight trigram symbol used by Taoism and practitioners of Feng Shui.

MMA DICTIONARY

Back Leg – Leg that is farthest from the opponent. The back leg is used to deliver the power kick which is why the strongest leg is the back leg.

Bando – Burmese armed and unarmed combat system utilizing karate and judo style techniques.

Bang – Slang for Fight.

Barai – Sweep in the Japanese language. *See Sweep.*

Bellator – Mixed Martial Arts league founded in Santa Monica, California in 2008. Owned by Viacom, Bellator is the 2nd largest MMA promotion in the United States, second to the Ultimate Fighting Championship.

MMA DICTIONARY

Belt Grip – A hold that uses the opponent's martial arts belt to control their body weight.

Bisping, Michael – Actor, sports analyst, and former UFC Men's Middleweight Champion. Bisping's character and personality boosted his popularity among MMA fans and he transferred this in to sports media.

Black Belt – Signifies a martial artist's expertise in a particular style; karate, judo, jujitsu, etc. A Black Belt is considered a sign of a certain level of understanding of the mechanics and applications of martial arts techniques in a specific martial arts style.

MMA DICTIONARY

Bodylock – Clinch technique used in grappling. Submission fighters and wrestlers frequently use the bodylock to inhibit the ability of the opponent to escape. The bodylock is an effective grappling technique for transitioning to a dominant position.

Body Slam – A takedown in which the attacker wraps their arms around the opponent, lifts them up, and brings them down to the floor with force.

Body Triangle – A body lock used by submission fighters while on the ground. The body triangle traps the opponents body with the attacker's legs, causing them to be trapped and exposed to submissions and striking.

MMA DICTIONARY

Bokken – Wooden sword in the Japanese language. The Bokken was used frequently for sword sparring by Japanese Samurai.

Bout – A legally sanctioned match between two amateur or professional opponents. Organized by a Fight Promoter.

Boxing – Western striking style that focuses on punching an opponent. All mixed martial artists use Boxing for striking with the hands. Boxing uses focus mitts, heavy bag, sparring, and running to train a professional fighter for competition. Boxing is one of the major styles of fighting that is incorporated in to an MMA fighter's style. Boxing has proven its effectiveness in MMA

MMA DICTIONARY

bouts as all MMA fighters use a variant of a Boxing punch when striking with their hands.

Brazilian Jiu-Jitsu – Brazilian martial art influenced by Pre-World War II Japanese Judo, that emphasizes ground grappling. Founded by Helio Gracie and Carlson Gracie Sr. Increased in popularity as BJJ fighters challenged

MMA DICTIONARY

fighters globally and with the creation of the UFC.

Briggs, Shannon – Two time Heavyweight Boxing Champion known for the iconic phrase "Let's Go Champ".

Broughton, John Jack - Bareknuckle Boxing Champion. Invented mufflers, which became the predecessor to the modern Boxing glove.

Budo – Martial Way in the Japanese language.

Bunkai – The applications of the kata in Japanese Karate.

MMA DICTIONARY

Bushi – Warrior in the Japanese language. The Bushi were a class of professional soldiers.

Bullshido – Satirical name given by legitimate Martial Artists to fake Martial Arts or fighting styles. *See McDojo.*

Bushido – Japanese Way of the Warrior.

Butterfly Guard – Open Guard used in BJJ. Your feet are placed against the thighs of the opponent and waist, controlling their posture. The butterfly guard is an effective guard because it focuses on attacking the opponent's waist and legs, disrupting their balance and their ability to effectively attack.

MMA DICTIONARY

C

Cage Fighting – Mixed Martial Arts competitions held within a caged area. Caged matches were frequently featured in professional wrestling competitions many years before MMA became popular.

Capoeira – Brazilian martial art that utilizes dance-like movements and focuses mainly on kicking techniques. Capoeira uses dynamic rather than static stances. Several UFC fighters including Anderson Silva and Jose Aldo use Capoeira in the octagon.

Cardio – Exercises that increase the athlete's respiratory system so that they do not "run out" of breath during

MMA DICTIONARY

competition. Cardio exercises increase an athlete's stamina and lung power. Cardio is considered the most important element of a fighter because without lung power and stamina, a fighter will lose the ability to defend themselves and/or to attack the opponent.

Catch Wrestling – Wrestling style that utilizes various submission techniques. American catch wrestling was made famous by professional wrestling leagues.

Cha Chuan – Chinese kung fu style developed by Muslims in the 14th century. Cha Chuan lead to several splinter styles being created including Tai Chi. *See Pai Chi.*

MMA DICTIONARY

Chagi – Kicking techniques in the Korean language.

Chi – Chinese language term for Internal Energy. Also known as Ki in the Korean and Japanese languages. Chi or Ki is a belief based in philosophy without any credible scientific data to prove its existence. Despite there being no evidence to prove their claims, there have been several "Chi Masters" that have claimed to be able to harness Chi to knockout an opponent without touching them.

Chi Kung – Also known as Chi Qong. Chinese breathing exercises used to stimulate blood circulation and to increase health.

MMA DICTIONARY

Chin-na – Chinese martial art that emphasizes trapping and locking techniques.

Chodan – Mid-level in the Japanese language.

Choke – Technique used in Judo, Catch Wrestling, and Jujitsu, that cuts off the oxygen to the opponent, forcing them to submit or lose consciousness. An individual will become unconscious in 5 seconds or less, therefore the practice of choking techniques should only be carried out under a highly skilled trainer or coach.

Clinch – Standing grappling position where your opponent is held by you giving you control over them.

MMA DICTIONARY

Closed Guard – Jujitsu guard used by defender laying on their back. The legs of the defender are wrapped around the waist to upper body, controlling the movement of the opponent. The closed guard is effective for effectively preventing the opponent from attacking.

Coach – A person that guides and teaches an MMA fighter. MMA coaches are highly paid and highly

MMA DICTIONARY

capable of preparing amateur and professional fighters for MMA competition.

Collar Choke – BJJ technique whereby an opponent's collar is used to choke the opponent.

Combatives – Hand to Hand fighting style used by the United States military. Combatives are influenced by Judo, Jujitsu, Karate, and self-defense techniques.

Commentator – An individual that narrates an MMA match. Famous fight commentators include Joe Rogan.

Competition – Strategic consideration that seeks rivalry and

MMA DICTIONARY

opposition rather than interdependence. In an MMA match, there is one winner and one loser. Two fighters are *competing* to win money and prestige.

Conditioning – Preparation of the body. MMA fighters use specialized conditioning coaches that prepare a fighter to have the stamina to compete in a professional MMA match. Conditioning, is many MMA fights, the defining factor between victory and loss.

Cormier, Daniel – Two time UFC Champion, Light Heavyweight and Heavyweight.

Counter – Technique used during an opponent's attack.

MMA DICTIONARY

Cyborg, Cris – UFC Women's Featherweight Champion. Aggressive powerful fighting style that uses Muay Thai and BJJ. She has been called the Female version of Wanderlei Silva for her ferocious and unrelenting fighting style.

D

Dachi – Stance.

Damriram, Jitti – World famous Muay Thai coach to professional MMA and Muay Thai fighters. Owner of the prestigious Jitti Gym in Bangkok, Thailand.

Dan – Ranking or level in the Japanese language. Ranking were created to award new students as

MMA DICTIONARY

well as to create an organization. Kano adapted the ranking system of belts from Gichin Funakoshi's Shotokan Karate.

Densho – Secret teaching in the Japanese language. Secret meaning passed down orally and not written down.

Dim mak – Vital point striking system that is believed to give the practitioner to be able to kill using one strike.

Dirty Boxing – Punching while in the Clinch position.

Do – Way in the Japanese language.

MMA DICTIONARY

Dojo – Training Hall. Literally "place of the way".

Dominant Position – A grappling position that allows for the application of strikes and submission techniques to an opponent while minimizing the risks of being attacked by an opponent.

Double Leg Takedown – Grappling takedown technique whereby the defender grabs both legs of the attacker, pulls the attacker's legs with both hands while applying pressure using their shoulder which is placed at the attacker's waist. A variant of the double leg takedown is the single leg takedown.

The double leg takedown has a high rate of success from mid to close distance, forcing the opponent on to

MMA DICTIONARY

their back and placing the defender in a dominant position. The double leg takedown is used by wrestlers, submission grapplers, Judo practitioners, and Jujitsu fighters.

Dozo – Japanese term for please.

Dumog – Filipino martial art that specializes in wrestling.

E

Eskrima – Filipino Martial Art that uses one or two eighteen-inch-long bamboo sticks. Eskrima was used by Filipino fighters in WW2 against invaders. Eskrima is a deadly art in the hands of a skilled practitioner.

MMA DICTIONARY

Empi – Elbow in the Japanese language. The empi is an effective powerful strike when used from a close distance. The empi is a strong striking technique that has the ability to knockout an opponent from close distance. The Empi or elbow strike is not exclusive to Karate as Muay Lao, Lethwei, and Muay Thai fighters use elbow techniques extensively.

MMA DICTIONARY

F

Fight – A professional or amateur match between two opponents engaging in combat sports.

Fighter – An individual that fights in a professional or amateur fight league, fighting competition, or fighting event for prestige and/or

MMA DICTIONARY

prize money. Fighters spend many years training and competing in order to hone and polish their skills for professional competition.

Fight Club – An informal training and sparring group.

Fight Contract – Contract between MMA promoter and fighter.

Fight Doctor – Trained medical professional that oversees the health of both fighters during an MMA match.

Fight Promoter – A person that organizes professional combat sports events. Dana White is a famous MMA fight promoter.

MMA DICTIONARY

Fighter – An amateur or professional that engages in combat sports for prestige and/or prize money. Fighters spend a considerable amount of time in training, keeping their body conditioned and prepared for their next competition.

Fish Hooking – An illegal technique in MMA in which a fighter sticks their hand in an opponent's mouth in order to control the head and body of the opponent.

Flanking – Maneuver that concentrates superior forces against a weaker force. MMA fighters use flanking techniques to avoid strikes and to attack the weak side of an opponent.

MMA DICTIONARY

Flying Knee – Jumping knee technique used by Muay Thai fighters and Karate practitioners. The flying knee has been used effectively in MMA competition.

Forfeit – Surrender by an opponent causing an immediate loss. If an opponent fails to show or fails to continue the fight they are forfeiting.

Foul – Illegal move that results in a penalty such as deduction of points and disqualification. An illegal blow or an illegal technique results in a foul. *For example, Fish Hooking is an illegal blow.*

Front Leg – Your leg that is closest to the opponent. The front leg is

MMA DICTIONARY

used to kick, sweep, trip, and knee the opponent.

Full Guard – Jujitsu position where you lock your legs around the opponent while you are laying on your back. This position allows you to control the opponent's waist thereby controlling their weight. *See Closed Guard*.

Fudoshin – Calm Mind in the Japanese language. It is a state of mind that is achieved through practice.

Full Mount – Wrestling, Judo, and Jujitsu position that places you on top of your opponent's chest, giving you complete control over them. The full mount is the most advantageous

MMA DICTIONARY

position because you are able to attack your opponent without your opponent being able to attack you. An attacker can easily apply multiple submission techniques from the full mount position.

Funakoshi, Gichin – Founder of Shotokan Karate. Gichin Funakoshi's student Sosai Masutatsu Oyama founded Kyokushin Karate. Funakoshi was able to receive official recognition and support from the Japanese Government for his Shotokan Karate.

G

Gedan – Low in the Japanese language. *For example, Mawashi*

MMA DICTIONARY

Gedan means "low kick" in the Japanese language.

Geri – Kick in the Japanese language.

Gi – Uniform in the Japanese language.

Glassjaw – A fighter with a weak chin that gets knocked out easily. This term was adapted in to MMA from the sport of Boxing. Fighters with a glassjaw are seen as unable to take multiple blows or are unable to withstand damage. Fighters with glassjaws may be matched up against brawlers or denied fights because of their perceived weakness. The ability to bear blows and absorb strikes is a vital skill for a

MMA DICTIONARY

Mixed Martial Artist. Mixed Martial Artists that lack the ability to take blows tend to have shorter and less successful careers.

MMA DICTIONARY

Gloves – Padded hand mitts used in MMA and Boxing to prevent injuries. MMA Gloves are lighter in weight in comparison to Boxing Gloves which feature thicker and heavier padding. Famous fighting gloves manufacturers include Everlast and Venum. Fighting gloves are believed to have evolved from the Roman cestus, a rudimentary hand wrapped glove used in Pankration. The boxing glove was invented by bare knuckle boxing champion John "Jack" Broughton (1703-1798). Jack Broughton created "mufflers" that were used for sparring. The padding in Broughton's gloves is what differentiated the "muffler" and the Roman "cestus". Although the Roman "cestus" was an ancient type of glove, it really consisted of leather

MMA DICTIONARY

wraps with protruding studded metal pieces attached. Broughton's "muffler" was uniquely different and its ability to reduce the impact of blows was readily apparent. The first time Broughton's gloves were used in a boxing match was in Aix-la-Chapelle, France in 1818. After the adoption of the Marquess of Queensberry Rules, the gloves that were adopted weighed 2 ounces or less. It was the boxing match between John L Sullivan and James J Corbett that popularized the 5 ounce boxing glove as this match was the first gloved Heavyweight Championship of the world.

MMA DICTIONARY

Go – Hard in the Japanese
language. Go is the opposite of "Ju"
which means Soft. Go or hard

MMA DICTIONARY

techniques are striking techniques such as punching or kicking.

G.O.A.T. – Greatest of all time. *For example, in the sport of Boxing, some view Muhammad Ali as the GOAT.*

Goju – Japanese (Karate) styles that incorporate both hard striking and soft submission techniques. Goju styles are a predecessor to Mixed Martial Arts and are based on Fujian White Crane Kung Fu. Goju styles blend striking and grappling in to forms and drills, allowing rapid muscle memorization through rote mastery of the movements.

Goshin – Japanese Self-defense techniques. Goshin Jujitsu consists

MMA DICTIONARY

of escape techniques, reversal
techniques, grappling techniques,
and evasion techniques.

Gracie, Carlson (Sr) – Co-founder
of Brazilian Jujitsu along with Helio
Gracie.

Gracie, Helio – Co-founder of
Brazilian Jujitsu. Issued the "Gracie
Challenge" to fighters globally and
took part in grappling matches
against any willing competitor.

Gracie, Royce – Brazilian Jiu-Jitsu
exponent that won the first UFC
Championship, making Brazilian Jiu-
Jitsu famous worldwide.

Gracie, Royler – Judo Black Belt.
Brazilian Jujitsu Black Belt. Award

MMA DICTIONARY

winning Grappler. Mixed Martial
Artist that has competed in high
profile competitions such as Pride.

Grand Strategy – Main strategy
from which strategic objectives and
implementation plans are derived.

Grappler – A fighter that specializes
in a grappling style such as BJJ,
Wrestling, Judo, Sumo, or Dumog.
Grapplers tend to have longer
careers in MMA in contrast to
strikers. Some Grapplers like Randy
Couture have enjoyed extensive
careers.

Grappling – Wrestling. Grappling
can be in a standing position or on
the ground (Ne-Waza in Japanese).
Grappling techniques focus on

MMA DICTIONARY

control and submission rather than striking.

Grips – Use of holds or grabs to secure an opponent's gi, wrist, lapel, or collar.

Ground and Pound – Style used by MMA fighters that focuses on takedowns and ground striking. Wrestlers and Pit Fighters have used this style with high success in the UFC.

Ground Game – Ground grappling also known as Ne Waza in Judo and Jujitsu. Brazilian Jujitsu focuses mostly on ground grappling.

MMA DICTIONARY

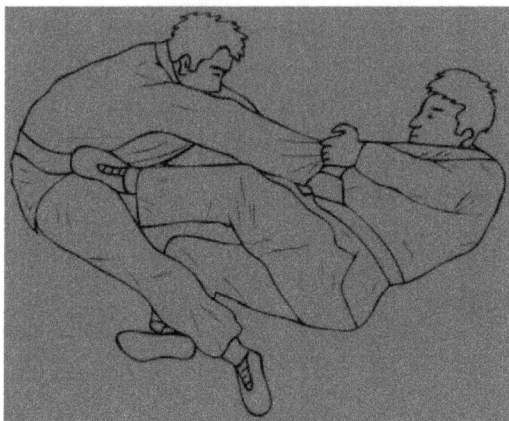

Guillotine – Submission technique that starts with the opponent being place in a front headlock. It is a standard submission technique used in MMA matches.

Gyaku Tsuki – Reverse punch in the Japanese language. It is a main tool in the striking arsenal of a Karate practitioner. The Gyaku Tsuki is used as a powerful knockout punch. Sosai Masutatsu Oyama

MMA DICTIONARY

frequently used the Gyaku Tsuki to knockout a 1 ton bull in demonstrations of strength. Gyaku Tsuki is a power strike used to knockout an opponent.

H

Hai – Japanese term for yes.

Hajime – Japanese term for beginning.

Half Guard – Jujitsu position where you lock your legs around one of the legs of your opponent while you are laying on your back.

Hapkido – Korean Martial Art that blends hard strikes with submission techniques. Hapkido kicking

MMA DICTIONARY

techniques are flashy and similar to Tae Kwan Do and its grappling techniques are similar to Japanese Jujitsu.

Hattori Hanzo – Famous Ninja. Leader of the Iga Ryu school of Ninjitsu. 1542-1596. 16th century Iga Ninja leader that saved Tokugawa Ieyasu after Oda Nobunaga's death. In one famous battle between Tokugawa and Takeda, Tokugawa was forced to retreat to his castle after taking heavy losses on the battlefield. Tokugawa had only five men left after this battle so he charged out beating a drum which saved him some time because the Takeda thought that this was a trap. In the middle of the night, Hattori Hanzo and his Ninjas crept in to the

MMA DICTIONARY

Takeda camp and wreaked havoc on them, causing the Takeda army encamped outside Tokugawa castle to flee. Hattori has been attributed with magical powers and referred to as being a Demon, but it was his perfect execution of operations and his meticulous planning rather than his fighting prowess, that gave him this nickname.

Haymaker – Punch thrown with little or no accuracy. Untrained street fighters are known to throw wild haymakers.

Heel Hook – Grappling submission technique focused on twisting and manipulating the ankle at the heel of the foot.

MMA DICTIONARY

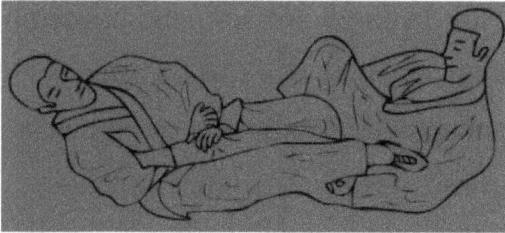

Helwani, Ariel – Famous MMA media personality known for up-close interviews with famous Mixed Martial Artists. Helwani has been able to successfully interview many MMA Champions and report on the state of the MMA industry.

Himitsu – Hidden techniques in the katas or forms. Many of the Katas in Karate are believed to have hidden techniques within them. It is believed that the hidden techniques hold the true Bunkai or Application of the technique. The Himitsu or Hidden

MMA DICTIONARY

techniques are believed to be hidden in order to protect the secrets of the movement.

Honbu – Headquarters. Main school in the Japanese language.

Hook – Boxing punching technique that uses the strength of the hips to generate force in a semi-circular motion. The hook is an effective and powerful punch that has the capability to knockout an opponent from close range.

Hook Kick – Kicking technique used in Tae Kwan Do that strikes at the opponent's face using a hooking motion. The hook kick surprises the opponent, making it difficult to defend against.

MMA DICTIONARY

The hook kick is an effective technique from close to mid-range.

Hug, Andy – Famous Kyokushin Karate practitioner known as the "blue eyed Samurai". Andy Hug was a popular proponent of Japanese Karate that was successful in many K1 competitions.

MMA DICTIONARY

Hyung – Form in the Korean language.

I

Iaido – The Japanese way of the sword.

Iga Ryu – Famous Japanese Ninjitsu school during Sengoku Jedai period. The Iga Ryu was famous for its many Ninja specializations and was hired by various Daimyo to carry out missions.

Illegal Techniques – Techniques that are not sanctioned for use in a particular bout or match. Illegal techniques include head-butting, fish hooking, and eye gouging. The use

MMA DICTIONARY

of illegal techniques results in infractions known as Penalties.

Inoki, Antonio – Japanese catch wrestler famous for competing against Boxing champion Muhammad Ali in a mixed martial arts competition. Inoki's match against Muhammad Ali was long and grueling, resulting in Muhammad Ali being taken to the hospital after the fight.

International Fight League – An MMA league that existed from 2006 to 2008. Team based MMA fights.

Ippon – Japanese term for a point scored in martial arts competition. Ippons are awarded based on the

MMA DICTIONARY

clean execution of a technique on an opponent.

J

Jeet Kun Do – Martial art created by Bruce Lee. Literally means "Way of the Intercepting Fist". Bruce Lee was heavily influenced by Wing Chun and Western Boxing, and thus created a style that incorporated elements of many styles. Some view Lee as an early pioneer of mixed martial arts because of his belief in not limiting oneself to any one particular style. Although Lee was a successful television and film actor, he slowly gained in popularity for his philosophical writings on the martial arts.

MMA DICTIONARY

Jiyu Kumite – Japanese term for Free Sparring.

Jitti Gym – Famous Muay Thai gym in Bangkok, Thailand that trains professional MMA and Muay Thai fighters.

MMA DICTIONARY

Jodan – Upper. Head & shoulders area.

Jojutsu – Japanese martial art system that uses a 4 foot (1.2m) long wooden staff.

Jones, Jon – Two time UFC Light Heavyweight Champion.

MMA DICTIONARY

Journeyman – Seasoned or veteran fighter with a few losses or more on their professional fight record. Journeymen were contenders that lost, resulting in losing ranking and/or sponsorship.

Ju – Soft. Pliable. Flexible. Yielding. Japanese language term.

MMA DICTIONARY

Judo – Japanese martial art and Olympic sport founded by Jigoro Kano in Japan. Judo, as created by Kano, was based on Kito-Ryu Jujitsu. Kito-Ryu Jujitsu focused on Standing Throwing techniques, which Kano adapted and added to create Judo. Kano added ground grappling to Judo and Ne Waza or ground grappling was the main focus of pre-WWII Judo. Kano was a technical fighter and focused on amalgamating the safer Jujitsu techniques in to the body of Judo. Kano was able to successfully recruit various martial arts teachers to learn Judo and to represent the style overseas. Judo grew widely in popularity when it was first introduced to the world through the Olympic Games. As pre-WWII Judo

MMA DICTIONARY

was focused on ground grappling or Ne Waza, Olympic organizers thought that this could tire the viewing audiences. Judo switched to focusing on standing throwing, in order to limit ground grappling and maintain an exciting watchable format.

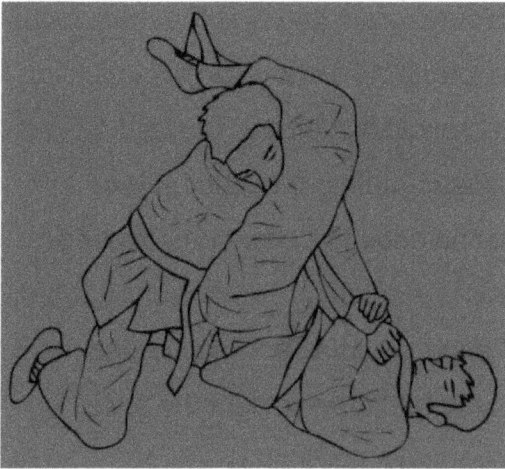

Juji-Gatame – Japanese term for Arm bar. The juji-gatame is referred

MMA DICTIONARY

to as an armbar in Brazilian Jujitsu. The juji-gatame is extensively used in Judo ground grappling (Ne-Waza).

Jujitsu – Japanese martial art that utilizes strikes, throws, locks, submission techniques, and ground grappling. Jujitsu is Japanese in origin, having evolved from the martial arts techniques used by the Samurai of Japan.

K

Kamae – Fighting stance in the Japanese language.

MMA DICTIONARY

Karate – An effective Martial Art that evolved in the Fukuoka islands situated between Japan and China. Karate arrived in Japan as Kenpo, which was the Japanese pronunciation for "Chuan Fa" or Kung Fu. Many Karate scholars believe that Karate was adapted

MMA DICTIONARY

from Chinese Foshan White Crane Kung Fu. The Bubishi, widely believed to be the authoritative book on Karate, was adopted from a Chinese book of military tactics authored by Wubei Zhi. The three main styles of Karate, as practiced in Japan, were Omari-Te, Shuri-Te, and Naha-Te. Modern Karate evolved from these three styles of Karate. Famous MMA Champions with Karate backgrounds include Georges St. Pierre, Lyota Machida, and Bas Rutten.

Kano, Jigoro – Founder of Judo and a Black Belt in Kito Ryu Jujitsu. Kano was heavily influenced by Jujitsu and picked out effective from Jujitsu and used them to form the style of Judo. Most of Judo's techniques are based

MMA DICTIONARY

on Kito Ryu Jujitsu, which was focused on Jujitsu throwing techniques. Kano was also influenced by Shotokan Karate founder Gichin Funakoshi, and adopted a Belt system to formalize Judo education.

Kata – Form or set of pre-defined movements that train the practitioners muscle memory. Kata is practiced at varying speeds, depending on the movements being executed.

Katana – Japanese long sword. The Katana was an important Samurai weapon that was deadly in the hands of a trained practitioner. The Katana was very sharp, being built using the finest craftsmanship and care.

MMA DICTIONARY

Kendo – Japanese sword fighting
sport martial art in which two
practitioners donning armor, use

MMA DICTIONARY

bamboo swords to defend and
attack. Kendo is believed to have
been derived from Kenjutsu or sword
techniques used by the Samurai.

MMA DICTIONARY

Keylock – Grappling submission technique whereby the defender grabs the wrist of the opponent and bends their arm at a 90 degree angle putting pressure on the opponent's shoulder. It is effective in a standing and ground position.

Ki – Japanese term for internal energy. Also spirit.

Kiai – Japanese Karate term for a yell used to generate energy and to distract opponent before, during, and after an offensive maneuver.

Kiba Datchi – Horse stance. This stance is believed to give its practitioner strong legs and a strong base for offensive maneuvers. Kiba Datchi is used frequently in both Tae

MMA DICTIONARY

Kwan Do and Karate. Kiba Dachi is a strong stance for delivering reverse punches, front kicks, and roundhouse kicks.

Kick Check – Blocking technique used to defend against a low kick. The defender raises their leg being attacked and deflects the incoming kick. The kick check has proven itself as an important and effective technique for preventing low kicks from an attacker. An attacker using a low kick against a defender using a kick check can result in pain or bone breakage for the attacker.

Kihon – Basics in the Japanese language.

MMA DICTIONARY

Kime – Focus or concentration in the Japanese language.

King, Don – Professional Boxing promoter that popularized the role of boxing promotion. Promoted many of Boxing champion Mike Tyson's professional bouts.

Knee On Stomach – Dominant grappling position used by Brazilian Jujitsu fighters to control their opponent while their opponent is laying on their back.

MMA DICTIONARY

Knee Shield – Position used by BJJ grapplers whereby the defender (laying on their back) uses their knee to prevent the attacker from passing the defender's guard. The defender laying on their back turns in towards the attacker.

Knee Strike – Standing striking technique used in various styles including Muay Thai and Karate. The knee strike can knockout or injure an opponent, which is why it has been banned in many kickboxing and MMA tournaments.

Knockdown – A strike that results in an opponent falling to the floor.

MMA DICTIONARY

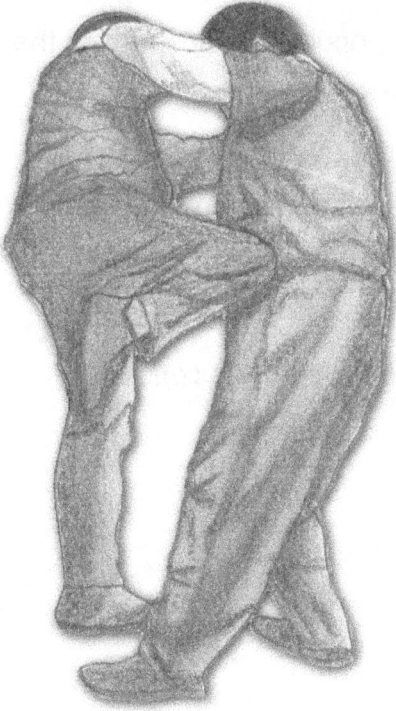

Knockdown Karate – Synonym for
Sosai Mas Oyama's style named
Kyokushin Karate, which focused on
hard low kicks delivered to the
opponent's legs. Oyama's

MMA DICTIONARY

Knockdown Karate style (Kyokushin) became popular fast because of the desire of Karate fighters to spar constantly. Oyama's Kyokushin Karate became even more popular than Gichin Funakoshi's Shotokan Karate, due to its insistence on fighting in every class session.

MMA DICTIONARY

Knockout – When an opponent has been knocked down and is unable to stand back up, the fight is ruled as a KO or knockout.

Koga Ryu – Famous Ninja school started by 53 families in the late 10th century that pioneered use of illusions and guerilla warfare. The Koga Ryu trained Ninja in various skills including hand to hand combat, climbing, infiltration, escape, illusion, and astronomy.

Kohai – Japanese term for a junior leader in a martial arts school or organization. The Kohai usually reports to a senior leader or Sempai.

Kokoro – Japanese term for heart.

MMA DICTIONARY

Krav Maga – Israeli martial art that uses effective techniques from multiple styles including judo, aikido, boxing, karate, and others.

Kudo – Japanese Mixed Martial Art style founded by Takashi Azuma. Kudo practitioners use punches, kicks, throws, grappling, ground fighting, and submission techniques. Kudo matches consist of two fighters competing using gloves and safety headgear. Kudo is practiced extensively in Russia, Japan, and Europe, with growing popularity in many developing and developed nations. Kudo is MMA with safety headgear and gloves to prevent injuries to the competitors.

MMA DICTIONARY

Kumiuchi – Ancient Japanese grappling art form. Thought to be the predecessor to Sumo and Japanese Jujitsu.

Kung Fu – Chinese martial art that encompasses hundreds of styles. Literally means "hard work". Kung Fu was popularized in Western film and cinema through movies and television shows. The mystique of the Shaolin Temple was popularized and commercialized through the use of mass media. Influential martial arts actors such as Jet Li, Jackie Chan, and Bruce Lee promoted and pushed Kung Fu to mass audiences via action movies.

MMA DICTIONARY

Kunoichi – Female Ninja during the
Sengoku Jedai period in Japan.
Skilled in climbing, surveillance, and
misinformation. Female Ninja used
multiple disguises and costumes to
infiltrate enemy castles.

MMA DICTIONARY

Kyokushin – Karate style that emphasizes low powerful kicks and powerful punches. Founded by Korean Sosai Mas Oyama. Kyokushin Karate gained greater popularity than Shotokan Karate because of Oyama's insistence on

MMA DICTIONARY

Jiyu Kumite. Sparring matches were legendary and very popular, attracting large numbers of students to Oyama's newly created Kyokushin Karate. Kyokushin Karate held many demonstrations and competed internationally against styles such as Muay Thai and Kickboxing in order to show its efficiency. Many other knockdown styles of Karate were directly created by students of Oyama.

Kyudo – Japanese martial art that utilizes the bow and arrow with a focus on character development. Kyudo is practiced in a meditation like manner that is thought to induce a Zen like state in the archer.

MMA DICTIONARY

L

Lao Tzu – Author of Tao Te Ching, a key book of Taoist philosophy. Lao

MMA DICTIONARY

Tzu influenced Taoist thought and presented it through his writings.

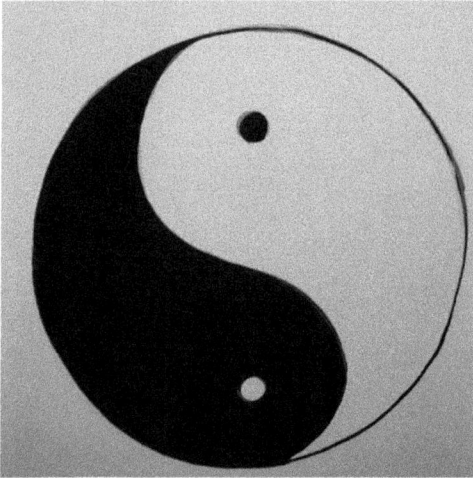

Lay and Pray – Term given for fighting style used by MMA fighters that seek to fall on their back and hope to submit their opponent from their back. This style is frequently used by individuals that are highly trained in Brazilian Jujitsu. Royce

MMA DICTIONARY

Gracie was a frequent user of this style and invited opponents to join him on the mat. It is also known as "pulling guard". Jujitsu use this method in order to position themselves in to a dominant position, allowing for a submission technique.

Lee, Bruce – Martial artist and actor that used a combination of various martial arts to create the style of Jeet Kun Do. Lee was popularized through television shows and movies. Lee is viewed by some martial artists as an actor and is viewed by some martial artists as the epitome of martial arts. Despite never having competed in any martial arts competition or tournament, Lee gained in popularity for his martial arts through the many

MMA DICTIONARY

films that he starred in. Lee was a student of Wing Chun master Ip Man, but did not complete his studies under Ip Man. Lee adopted the techniques he did learn and absorbed them in to a new style he created, known as Jeet Kun Do. There are many stories of Lee having been a street fighter in Hong Kong. Lee started teaching Americans the techniques of Chinese martial arts and was forced to fight Hong Man Jack in order to uphold his right to teach them. Lee lost in the no holds barred fight to Hong Man Jack and was hospitalized. Lee created Jeet Kun Do during this period and upon recovery, opened his first school, teaching hundreds of students his newly created style.

MMA DICTIONARY

Leg Locks – Jujitsu techniques that attack the legs of the opponent in order to force a submission. Submission fighters specialize in the use of leg locks as they are difficult to defend against.

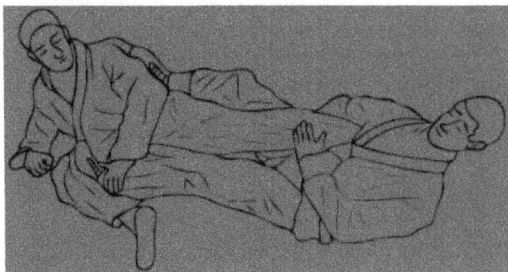

Lesnar, Brock – Former UFC undisputed Heavyweight Champion.

Lethwei – Cambodian martial art similar to Muay Thai.

MMA DICTIONARY

Losing – Failing to meet objectives. A fighter can lose in a myriad of ways including TKO and submission.

Lua – Hawaiian martial art that specializes in bone breaking techniques.

Lumberjack Sweep – BJJ sweep used against an attacker whereby the defender pulls both ankles of the attacker while applying pressure to the hips.

Luring – Tactic that draws the opponent in causing them to be ambushed.

Luta Livre – Brazilian martial art started in the 1920's. Mixture of wrestling, jujitsu, and striking

MMA DICTIONARY

techniques. Rival of Brazilian Jujitsu.
Believed to be a predecessor of
Mixed Martial Arts.

M

Mae – Front in the Japanese
language.

Mae Geri – Front kick in Japanese.
Mae Geri is an effective kicking

MMA DICTIONARY

technique that can generate immense power. The Mae Geri can be used as a strike or as a push, depending on the tactic being used. The Mae Geri has a high probability of landing on an opponent and is difficult to defend against because of its straight line attack.

Mae Ai – Distance in the Japanese language. Mae Ai is used by Karate fighters in sparring or Jiyu Kumite to create distance between themselves and the opponent. The constant distancing movement creates an opportunity for attacking the opponent. Conor Mcgregor is an MMA fighter that is able to use distance effectively.

MMA DICTIONARY

Machida, Lyota – Shotokan Karate proponent. Former UFC Light Heavyweight Champion. Proved the value and effectiveness of Karate in the Octagon by defeating several mixed martial arts champions.

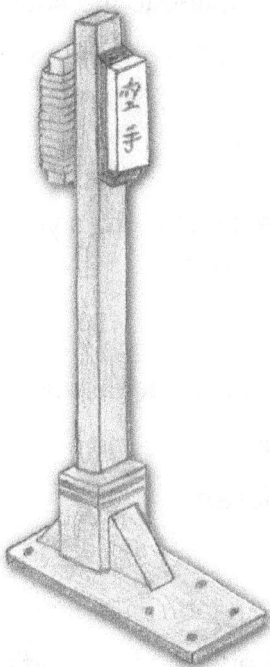

MMA DICTIONARY

Makiwara – Wooden striking post used in Karate. A makiwara is used for building strength in the Karate fighter and to increase their striking power. A makiwara can be round or square with a padded striking pad consisting of foam or rope. A makiwara can be bolted to the floor or buried partially in the ground to add stability.

Maneuver – A tactic that gives you an advantage.

Martial Art – A system of unarmed or armed combat. *For example, Karate is a martial art.*

Martial Artist – An individual that practices martial arts. A martial artist

MMA DICTIONARY

practices a code inside and outside the martial arts school.

Martial Arts – The umbrella term for all of the martial arts including armed and unarmed combat techniques.

Mayweather, Floyd – Famous American undefeated Boxing champion. Retired undefeated with fifty wins and zero losses. Famous for his antics inside and outside the ring. Mayweather is one of the highest paid athletes on earth having generated hundreds of millions of dollars in professional Boxing.

McDojo – Satirical name given to martial arts school that churn out Black Belts without fighting skill. *See Bullshido.*

MMA DICTIONARY

McGregor, Conor – Irish Mixed Martial Artist. Two time UFC Champion. Famously competed against Floyd Mayweather Jr. in a Boxing match.

Mixed Martial Arts – The umbrella term for Martial Arts competitions that utilize varying styles. The most famous of the MMA or Mixed Martial Arts leagues is the UFC or Ultimate Fighting Championships. The UFC lead the drive to legitimize Mixed Martial Arts in the view of State officials and law enforcement. The popularization of MMA was lead by Dana White through the UFC.

Match – A licensed or unlicensed fight between two opponents engaging in combat sports. Each

MMA DICTIONARY

combat sports event can feature several matches in a single day or night. The slot for a match is paid for by the fight promoter. The fighters in a match are most likely discovered by a matchmaker and hired by the fight promoter. A match is usually sanctioned by an Athletic Commission.

Matchmaker – An individual that organizes a match between two opponents. Matchmakers are usually independent and are contracted by fight promoters to find fighters for a specific combat sports event.

Matte – Stop in the Japanese language. Matte is used as a verbal command by a Karate instructor to

MMA DICTIONARY

alert a student or students that they must stop immediately.

Mawate – Turn Around in the Japanese language. Mawate is used as a verbal command by a Karate instructor to alert students that they must turn around.

Mikazuki Geri – Crescent Kick in the Japanese language. The Mikazuki Geri is used from a short to mid range to attack the head and upper body of the opponent. It is an effective technique because its delivery makes its defense difficult.

MMA – Mixed Martial Arts. There are many theories as to who created mixed martial arts, but its progression was fueled by the

MMA DICTIONARY

success of the Ultimate Fighting Championship. Mixed Martial Arts went from being viewed as an illegal business to becoming a multi-billion dollar global business. From merchandising deals to various licensing deals, the UFC has been able to greatly capitalize on its industry leadership.

MMA Gym – Gym that focuses on the teaching and training of MMA fighters. Xtreme Couture (Randy Couture) and UFC Gym are two examples of MMA gyms.

MMA Promoter – Fight promoter that specializes in organizing and funding Mixed Martial Arts competitions. Famous MMA promoters include Dana White.

MMA DICTIONARY

MMA Promotion – An event that features MMA matches. An MMA promotion can be amateur or professional, free or ticketed, and sanctioned or not sanctioned. The most famous MMA promotion is that of the UFC and then Bellator MMA.

Mobility – Tactical movements designed to keep the opponent off balance and at a disadvantage. Fighters with greater mobility are able to outmaneuver their opponents and create openings to attack. A fighter that lacks mobility allows their opponent to attack them with greater ease. Lyota Machida and Conor Mcgregor are two examples of MMA fighters that have excellent mobility. Mobility assists in the offensive and defensive techniques of a fighter, allowing them an advantage in position and timing.

Mochizuke Chiyomi – Female Ninja. Created a school of 300 female Ninjas in Koga. The Koga ninjas were famous for their meticulous planning and precise execution.

MMA DICTIONARY

Mokuso – Meditation in the Japanese language. Mokuso is frequently used by Karate practitioners in order to relax their mind. Mokuso meditation can be used before a match to calm the mind of the fighter or it can be used after a training session. Mokuso relaxes the Karate practitioner,

MMA DICTIONARY

allowing them to be able to think clearly in competition.

Morehei Ueshiba – Student of Sokaku Takeda. Founded Aikido or Way of Peace. Ueshiba incorporated the movements of Kendo and Jujitsu, creating an effective unarmed system of combat that went on to be used by Japanese Police. Ueshiba promoted the Way of Peace as the official mantra of Aikido.

Muay Boran – Native Thai Martial Art that practices Muay Thai as a traditional martial art rather than as a combat sport. Muay Boran is believed to be the predecessor of Muay Thai. Some believe that Muay Boran is Cambodian in origin and others argue that Muay Boran is

MMA DICTIONARY

originally from Laos. The similarities between Muay Lao, Lethwei, and Muay Boran are numerous.

Muay Lao – Laotian Martial Art thought to be the influencer of Muay Thai. Muay Lao, Lethwei, and Muay Boran share many similarities.

Muay Thai – Thai Kickboxing. Muay Thai's predecessor Muay Boran was influenced by Muay Lao. It is believed that Muay Thai was brought from Laos to Thailand in the 19th century. Muay Thai is seen as the National Sport of Thailand and Thailand attracts thousands of tourists per year looking to train authentic Muay Thai. Muay Thai is known as the "Art of 8 Limbs" and its techniques are highly effective in

MMA DICTIONARY

both K1 kickboxing style competitions as well as in Mixed Martial Arts competitions. The top Muay Thai gyms in Thailand cater to both professional Thai and foreign fighters. Muay Thai gyms are simple and humble, with a boxing ring and a few heavy bags. Muay Thai fighters spend most of their training on Focus Mitts and Sparring.

Musashi, Miyamoto – Self-taught master swordsman in Japan that dueled 60 times victoriously. Author of the Book of Five Rings. Musashi popularized his own style of sword fighting. Musashi engaged in several famous duels and established a school to teach his martial way. Musashi in his Book of Five Rings said "There is timing in everything.

MMA DICTIONARY

Timing in strategy cannot be mastered without a great deal of practice.

Timing is important in dancing and pipe or string music, for they are in rhythm only if the timing is correct. Timing and rhythm are also involved

MMA DICTIONARY

in the military arts, shooting bows
and guns, and riding horses. In all
skills and abilities there is timing.
There is also timing in the Void.
There is timing in the whole life of
the warrior, in his thriving and
declining, in his harmony and
discord."

N

MMA DICTIONARY

Nage – Throwing in the Japanese language.

Ng Mui – Founder of the style that evolved into Wing Chun. Wing Chun is a traditional Chinese martial art that was founded based on the principles of the Shaolin Temple. Ng Mui taught the style to a woman named Wing Chun, who went on to propagate the style.

Ninja – Japanese mercenary assassins that were expertly trained in stealth techniques including the murdering their opponents in their sleep. The ninja of Japan were trained in several skills and they included hand to hand combat as well as illusion. The Ninja would create formalized contracts with their

MMA DICTIONARY

employers and were sworn to lifelong secrecy. The Ninja not only carried out assassinations but also collected information, infiltrated enemy lands to sow dissent, and carried out various tasks for pay.

The Ninja of Iga province were the most famous and well trained Ninja practitioners and created a

MMA DICTIONARY

formalized Ninja school for training top level Ninjas. Female Ninjas were prevalent and carried out assassinations as well or better than their male counterparts. Female Ninjas used various disguises and costumes to easily penetrate an enemy castle and dispatch a target of assassination.

Ninjitsu – Japanese martial art that emphasizes silent attacks, invisibility, and evasions. Started in the late 10th century when the study of Guerrilla Warfare mixed with the study of Illusions. Ninjitsu incorporates various skills and techniques in its practitioner. *See Ninja.*

No Holds Barred – Mixed Martial Arts form of competition that has little

MMA DICTIONARY

or no rules. The early UFC was heavily influenced by No Holds Barred competitions. Pit Fighting contests and Vale Tudo competitions are examples of no holds barred fighting. No Holds Barred competitions can be dangerous, violent, and bloody because of their lack of rules. Vale Tudo fights more frequently result in knockouts than submission finishes. *See Vale Tudo.*

Norris, Chuck – American Karate practitioner and actor. Famous for his many roles in martial arts movies and television shows.

North South Position – Position used by a grappler in which the opponent's head is placed within the legs of the defender while the

MMA DICTIONARY

defender's head is placed on the opponent's stomach. It is a dominant position used by grapplers for establishing control.

No Touch Martial Arts – Fake martial arts that claims to be able to knockout an opponent without touching them.

Nurmagomedov, Khabib – UFC Men's Lightweight Champion.

MMA DICTIONARY

Holds the record for the longest winning streak in UFC history and features a career with no losses.

O

Octagon – 8 sided ring first introduced and made popular by the Ultimate Fighting Championships.

Oi – Lunge in the Japanese language.

Okinawa – Birthplace of Karate.

Omaplata – BJJ ground grappling submission technique similar to a Key Lock. The defender, while laying on their back, puts their leg under the opponent's arm wrapping around their arm, and turns 180 degrees

MMA DICTIONARY

causing the opponent's arm to become entangled.

Open Guard – Jujitsu position that is used to control the opponent while you are on your back. The legs are not locked around the opponent but are kept open to be able to counter the offensive maneuvers of your opponent. The open guard has many variations but they are all effectively used to prevent an opponent from attacking.

Opponent Analysis – Study of the opponent and their strengths and weaknesses. Fighters routinely watch videos of their opponent to gain an advantage in the ring.

MMA DICTIONARY

O Soto Gari – Judo trip takedown used frequently in MMA competitions. The O Soto Gari uses the defender's momentum and leverage to force the attacker to the ground.

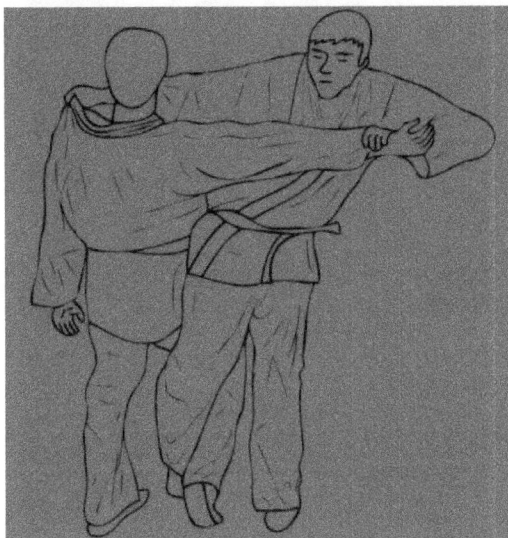

The defender's hands grabs the left lapel and right sleeve of the attacker while applying pressure to the left leg of the attacker. Using the push and pull method, the defender is able to

MMA DICTIONARY

takedown larger opponents. The
defender's forward momentum
provides the necessary force to bring
the attacker to the floor.

Osu – Greetings and respect in the
Japanese language.

MMA DICTIONARY

P

Pahlavani – Iranian traditional martial art based on ancient wrestling and grappling.

Pai Chi – Muslim Kung Fu. Known as Pai Chi Kon. Known as the external form of Tai Chi.

Pankration – Ancient Greek martial art that used wrestling, throws, and striking techniques. It is thought of as a predecessor to modern MMA. It was believed to be the most widely popular sport of the ancient Olympics.

Parry – Deflect. Parrying techniques are used to deflect or divert the attack of your opponent rather than

MMA DICTIONARY

to block and absorb the opponent's strike.

Pass – Passing the opponent's guard.

Penalty – An infraction that requires the deduction of points. Penalties can be awarded based on holding, stalling, or illegal techniques.

Pit Fighter – No Holds Barred type fighter that competes in pit fighting competitions for prize money. Pit Fighters like Tank Abbott are known to be among the strongest and toughest fighters because they are experienced in fights with no rules.

Pit Fighting – No Holds Barred style competition held on dirt, sand, grass,

MMA DICTIONARY

or concrete. Pit Fighting allows all techniques to be used including head-butting.

Pride – MMA competition league that originated in Japan. Competitions were held in a standard Boxing ring. Pride Fighting Championships featured highly seasoned professional fighters competing for prestige, bragging rights, and prize money. The Pride Fighting Championships was purchased by the UFC.

Promoter – Fight Promoter. Funds matches between two opponents for financial gain. Promoter uses the matchmaker to source the fighters. A fight promoter funds combat sports events and organizes them. The

MMA DICTIONARY

promoter profits by selling streaming video rights, selling tickets, selling concessions, and selling merchandise. Fight promoters gain the most from a combat sports event but also take the largest risk by funding it. Famous MMA Fight Promoters include Dana White.

R

Randori – Free Sparring in the Japanese language. Randori is most commonly practiced in Judo.

Rapidity – Speed in deployment and implementation of strategies.

Rear Naked Choke – A submission technique used by submission grapplers to submit an opponent.

MMA DICTIONARY

The arms form a triangle with one arm's forearm bending inwards to tighten the choke. The rear naked choke is used when a defender is able to position themselves behind the back of the opponent.

Referee – An individual authorized to officiate a professional or amateur combat sports match.

Regulated – Competitions that are sanctioned by an official State or Federal Athletic Commission.

Rei – Bow in the Japanese language. The Rei is performed as a greeting to a higher ranked student or instructor and as a sign of respect when entering or exiting a Dojo.

MMA DICTIONARY

Re-match – A competition that is held to decide who is the greater fighter, after one fighter has previously defeated the other. A re-match is usually agreed to beforehand and is included in a fight contract between two high profile fighters.

Reverse Punch – Powerful Karate punching technique. Referred to as a Cross Punch in Boxing. The reverse punch generates an immense amount of force, giving its user the ability knockout an opponent with a single strike.

MMA DICTIONARY

Rhee, Simon – 7th degree Tae Kwan Do Black Belt. Stunt and fight choreographer. Martial Arts actor.

Ring – Area in which a competition takes place. A ring, usually elevated and square, consists of 4 stakes or ring posts, with 3 ropes or more connecting the 4 corners.

Ring Magazine – Famous Boxing magazine that is widely read among

MMA DICTIONARY

Boxing fans. Ring Magazine was purchased by Golden Boy Promotions co-founder Oscar De La Hoya. Ring Magazine rates and reports on the professional Boxing industry.

Ring Rust – Refers to a fighter that has not been in the ring to fight in a long period of time.

Rockhold, Luke – Former UFC Middleweight Champion and Strikeforce Middleweight Champion.

Rogan, Joe – Famous MMA fight commentator, commentator, and TV/radio personality. Tae Kwan Do Black Belt. BJJ Black Belt.

MMA DICTIONARY

Ronin – A samurai that has been dismissed from service by his master or has become without a leader due to the death of his master. Ronin were frequently hired by Daimyo to carry out various tasks for compensation.

Roundhouse – Kicking technique used in Karate, Muay Thai, and Kickboxing. The roundhouse kick has the ability to generate an immense amount of force using a whip like motion of the leg. MMA fighters have been knocked out from sustaining too many kicks to their legs during a fight. The roundhouse kick is a standard tool in an MMA fighter's repertoire of fighting techniques.

MMA DICTIONARY

Rousey, Ronda – Judo Black Belt, Olympic Judo Medalist, and first UFC Women's Bantamweight Champion.

Ruas, Marco – Vale Tudo fighter. UFC Champion. MMA coach for Pedro Rizzo and others.

MMA DICTIONARY

Rufus, Rick – Famous American Kickboxer that popularized Kickboxing through his many championship victories.

Rutten, Bas – Famous MMA exponent, commentator, and fighter. Known for the Bas Rutten liver shot, a devastating body strike used to knockout an opponent.

Ryu – Japanese term for academy or school. A Ryu features a Sensei that teaches martial arts techniques.

S

Sabaki – Movement in the Japanese language. *For example, Tai Sabaki or Tae Sabaki is the circular movement around an opponent.*

MMA DICTIONARY

Sakuraba – Kazushi Sakuraba. Japanese catch wrestler that famously defeated Royce Gracie, Renzo Gracie, and Royler Gracie in the Pride Fighting Championships.

Sambo – Russian martial art influenced by judo, boxing, karate, and wrestling. Sambo was an official military martial art during the existence of the Soviet Union. MMA fighters with a Sambo backround have been very successful.

Samurai – Feudal class of warriors during 15th century Japan. Trained in armed and unarmed combat using long swords, bows, spears, short swords, and pikes. The samurai reported to a Daimyo or Feudal Warlord that controlled large areas of

MMA DICTIONARY

land. Samurai practiced several unarmed forms of combat including Jujitsu. Their techniques influenced various schools to teach "the Way of the Samurai" and the unarmed techniques they practiced.

MMA DICTIONARY

Sanda – Chinese full contact mixed martial art that combines Boxing, Kickboxing, and Throws. Also known as Sanshou. Sanda competitions are highly organized in China and feature fast paced sports combat athletes.

Sapp, Bob – Former NFL Football player. K1 Champion. Pride MMA competitor. Famous for his aggressive bullying fighting style.

Savate – French kickboxing sport.
Scissor Choke – Ground grappling submission technique whereby the defender traps the opponent's head between their legs and squeezes. It is not an efficient submission technique but it has been used frequently in MMA competition.

MMA DICTIONARY

Scissor Takedown – Jumping takedown used from a standing position whereby the attacker traps the opponent's legs with a scissor like motion and squeezes their legs causing the opponent to fall to the floor. The scissor takedown has varying degrees of success but it is used frequently in MMA competition.

Seagal, Steven – Famous 7th Dan Aikido master that trained and taught in Japan. Seagal speaks Japanese fluently and has starred in several high grossing movies.

Seiza – Japanese term for kneeling position.

Sempai – Senior leader in a martial arts school or organization. The

MMA DICTIONARY

Sempai usually reports to the Sensei.

Sensei – Instructor in the Japanese language. A Karate instructor is referred to as Sensei by their students.

Seppuku – Ritual of disembowelment carried out by samurai. It is also known as Hara Giri. It was done by Samurais that felt shame for having failed or having been defeated. It was also done under the order of a Daimyo for having committed an offense.

Shaolin Temple – Martial arts religious organization in China that spawned several fighting styles

MMA DICTIONARY

including 5 Animal Styles, Wing Chun, White Crane, and others.

Shuai Chiao – Chinese wrestling.

Shuriken – Ninja throwing star used in both China and Japan. The Shuriken were used by Ninja of Japan to dispatch an enemy from a distance during an infiltration or to delay a guard during escape.

MMA DICTIONARY

Shooto – Japanese grappling martial art based on shoot wrestling. Shooto was developed from the styles used in Japanese professional wrestling leagues.

Shoot Wrestling – An American grappling style based on catch wrestling techniques used in professional wrestling leagues. Shoot wrestling incorporated grappling, throws, takedowns, submission techniques, and striking. Shoot wrestling is viewed as an early predecessor of Mixed Martial Arts.

Shot – Term used for a grappler that attempts to takedown an opponent's legs.

MMA DICTIONARY

Shuto – Hand tensed in a rigid form similar to a knife. Shuto can be applied to the opponent's neck as a form of atemi.

Side Kick – Effective kicking technique used in Kung Fu, Karate, and Tae Kwan Do. The side kick uses a powerful thrusting motion that can generate over 1000 PSI of force.

MMA DICTIONARY

Sifu – Kung Fu Master. Although the Sifu is in charge of a Chinese martial arts school, they do not always teach, but rather assign higher ranked students teaching roles.

Silva, Wanderlei – MMA champion that earned the nickname "The Axe Murderer" for his aggressive fighting style. Specializes in Chute Box, which combines striking and

MMA DICTIONARY

grappling. Silva defeated tough opponents like Chael Sonnen and others to earn a reputation as a "no-nonsense" brawler. Although Silva is well trained in Brazilian Jujitsu, Silva prefers to dispatch opponents in a standing position with knees, elbows, and kicks.

Sleeve and Collar – The two main grips used simultaneously by BJJ grapplers in order to control an opponent. By grabbing the sleeve and collar of the opponent and applying the push and pull technique, a defender is able control the attacker.

Soto Uke – Japanese term for Outer hook block.

MMA DICTIONARY

Spider Guard – Jujitsu guard used
by defender laying on their back to
defend against opponent. The legs
of the defender are not locked
around the opponent, but rather
open. The defender uses their legs
and feet to attack the arms, throat,
and legs of the opponent.

MMA DICTIONARY

Sprawl – Standing grappling technique that is used to counter a takedown attempt. The defender shoots the hips out preventing the attacker from controlling the defender's hips, stopping the takedown.

Sprawl and Brawl – MMA style that focuses on preventing takedowns and keeping the fight in a standing position. MMA fighters that are skilled in Boxing and Striking techniques prefer to use the sprawl and brawl style of fighting.

MMA DICTIONARY

Stalling – Delaying tactic used by
Mixed Martial Artists in order to
prevent any scoring by an opponent.
Stalling is penalized and repeated
used of it can result in a
disqualification. An MMA fighter

MMA DICTIONARY

ahead in points may attempt to stall in the octagon in order to prevent an opponent from scoring.

Stand and Bang – MMA style that focuses on standing fighting.

Standing Grappling – Grappling techniques including submissions, throws, trips, and takedowns that are used from a standing position.

MMA DICTIONARY

St. Pierre, Georges – Three time UFC Champion. Kyokushin Karate practitioner. St Pierre is an extremely popular Mixed Martial Artist and has used his skills to position himself as one of the greatest MMA fighters of all time.

Strategic Advantage – An advantage that is gained and exploited in a competition or conflict. Positioning is a form of gaining strategic advantage. By positioning oneself in a position where the opponent can be attacked but is unable to attack you, you are able to gain a strategic advantage.

Strategic Objective – An objective that must be completed in order for

MMA DICTIONARY

the main objective or Grand Objective to be reached.

Strategy – Ways, Means, and Ends to an objective or objectives. *For example, Mark Hunt's strategy was to submit his opponent.*

Submission – Technique used to force your opponent to quit. Submission techniques are used in combination with grappling. The opponent submits by tapping their hands on the opponent's back or tapping their hands on the ground or by signaling the referee. An opponent can also submit by refusing to leave their corner or by throwing in the towel.

MMA DICTIONARY

Submission Combinations – The use of submission techniques in sequential order.

Submission Fighter – Fighter that focuses on takedowns and submission techniques. Submission fighters seek to avoid standing fighting and seek to clinch their opponent. From the clinch position, a submission fighter utilizes various trips, throws, and takedowns to cause an opponent to fall to the floor. From there, the submission fighter will use their advanced knowledge of submissions and ground fighting in order to achieve an advantageous position for applying a submission. *For example, Ken Shamrock is a Submission Fighter.*

MMA DICTIONARY

Submission Grappling – MMA fighting style famously used by Ken Shamrock and other MMA Champions. Focuses on throwing, pinning, and locking techniques. Although submission grappling proponents use striking, they tend to focus on grappling more.

Submission Techniques – Techniques that include choking, joint locks, joint manipulation, and pinning. Submission techniques are used in submission grappling styles such as Jujitsu or Judo. Submission techniques are most effective when used in sequence and in combinations. Submission grapplers tend to have long careers.

MMA DICTIONARY

Sumo – Japanese Wrestling martial art. It is thought to be the original Japanese martial art and there are several drawings which show Sumo to be nearly two thousand years old. Sumo is the national sport of Japan and its rituals and methods are ceremonial. Sumo techniques include simple striking techniques such as the palm strike to the opponent's chin.

MMA DICTIONARY

Sun Tzu – Chinese military strategist that pioneered and authored the Art of War. Sun Tzu is quoted often by martial artists and strategists because of his deep understanding of tactics and strategy. Sun Tzu argued for well-planned decision making and methods of organization. His book, the Art of War, is studied as a manual of combat.

MMA DICTIONARY

Superman – Punching technique that throws the body and the punching arm forward in a single leaping motion. The Superman Punch is delivered in a jumping overhead form so as to avoid the defense of the opponent. Frequently used in kickboxing and MMA matches. Georges St. Pierre is a proponent of the Superman Punch technique.

Sweat Box – MMA gym with poor ventilation.

MMA DICTIONARY

Sweep – Technique that causes the
opponent to lose their balance.
Usually implies your foot striking the
opponent's foot or ankle in such a
way that causes the opponent to
lose balance. Standard technique
used in Muay Thai and in Japanese
Karate. The sweep is effective

MMA DICTIONARY

against taller opponents and easy to apply from a short range.

Systema – Russian Military Special Forces martial art created for effectiveness.

MMA DICTIONARY

T

Tactics – Actions that implement strategy.

Taekwondo - Korean martial art and Olympic sport that emphasizes high kicks and jumping kicks. Famous practitioners include celebrated fight

MMA DICTIONARY

choreographer Simon Rhee and fight commentator Joe Rogan. Tae Kwan Do has been effectively used in MMA competition by various Mixed Martial Artists.

Tai Chi – Chinese Martial arts system used for meditation and health by increasing blood circulation. Tai Chi is practiced in over hundred nations on earth and is used as a supplementary health exercise. It is also a Kung Fu style that emphasizes evading and controlling the opponent in a counter-attack format. Also known as Taijiquan. Although Tai Chi is used for increasing blood circulation and for health purposes, it has a fighting style within its movements that are quite effective.

MMA DICTIONARY

Tai Sabaki – Japanese term for Circling and body shifting. It is mostly used by Karate practitioners to create openings in an opponent's defense. Tai Sabaki can be used effectively to off balance an opponent and to disrupt their rhythm. Tai Sabaki is used by Karate practitioners before striking an opponent.

Takeda, Sokaku – Japanese Daito Ryu Jujitsu master and teacher of Morehei Ueshiba, the founder of Aikido.

Takedown – Wresting and grappling technique used to bring the opponent to the ground. Takedown techniques are usually focused around the mid-section and legs of

MMA DICTIONARY

an opponent. Single leg, double leg, and hip takedowns are common in MMA matches.

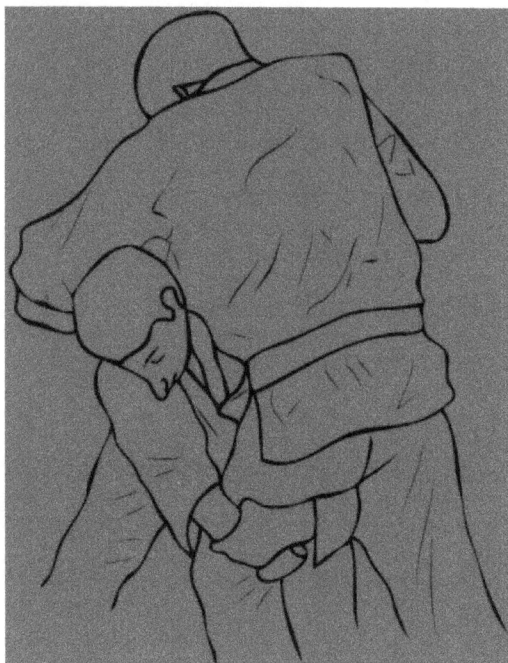

Tan Tien – Stomach in the Chinese language. Lower abdomen.

MMA DICTIONARY

Tap out – Term made popular by MMA competitions and used when an opponent submits in a competition or match. An opponent can signal verbally that they are tapping out or they can slap the ground 3 times.

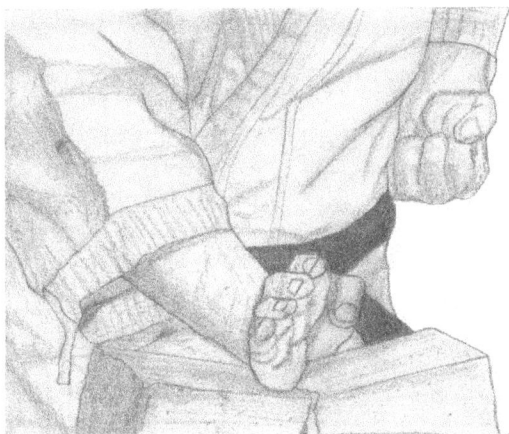

Tao – Chinese for "the Way". The philosophy of dualism. The Tao is

MMA DICTIONARY

symbolized by the Yin and Yang symbol. *See Lao Tzu.*

Tatami – Japanese term for a training Mat that was originally made from straw. Modern MMA gyms feature thick Tatami mats in their grappling areas.

Tate, Miesha – Defeated Holly Holm to become the UFC Women's Bantamweight Champion. Effective fighting style that focuses on wrestling and BJJ.

Teep – Front Kick in the Thai language. Refers to a push like kick used in Muay Thai. The teep is an effective technique for creating distance between yourself and the opponent.

MMA DICTIONARY

Title – A sanctioned Championship Belt in a specific weight class and league.

TKO – Technical Knockout. Stoppage of a fight due to the opponent being knocked down three times or because of injury. The referee will immediately stop the fight and issue a TKO because of an injury such as excess bleeding.

Tobi – Jumping in the Japanese language.

Tobi Geri – Jumping kick in the Japanese language. Tobi Mae Geri or Jumping Front Kick is an example of Tobi Geri.

MMA DICTIONARY

Toe Hold – Ground grappling technique applied to an opponent's toe causing them to submit.

Tornado Kick – A forward jumping spinning kick that is used in Capoeira and Tae Kwan Do. The tornado kick has been used by MMA champions including Conor Mcgregor. The tornado kick generates immense force from the spinning rotation of the kicker and is able to surprise an opponent with its rapidity.

Trainer – An individual with the capable experience to teach fighting skills to amateur and/or professional fighters. Trainers used focus mitts, heavy bag, jump rope, speed bag, and drills to teach skills to a fighter.

MMA DICTIONARY

Trip – Standing grappling technique that causes the opponent to fall to the floor. Effectively used within an opponent's clinch, Trips are used by BJJ fighters, Judo grapplers, and Wrestlers. Trips are effective because they depend on leverage rather than force.

Tsunetomo, Yamamoto – Author of the Hagakure and proponent of the Samurai code. Tsunetomo served as

MMA DICTIONARY

a retainer for the Nabeshima Clan and had firsthand knowledge of the Way of the Samurai. His writings were a journal of his observations while working and living as a Samurai retainer. His book, the Hagakure, is viewed as an informal manual on the Way of the Samurai. His writings are read by proponents of Japanese martial arts and Japanese Bushido. Tsunetomo was practically unknown in Japan until Western authors translated pieces of his Hagakure.

Tyson, Mike – Former Heavyweight Boxing Champion, Boxing Promoter, and student of legendary Boxing Trainer Cus D'Amato. Tyson generated over four hundred million dollars in his fighting career and

MMA DICTIONARY

influenced future generations of
Boxing.

U

Uchi – Inner in the Japanese
language.

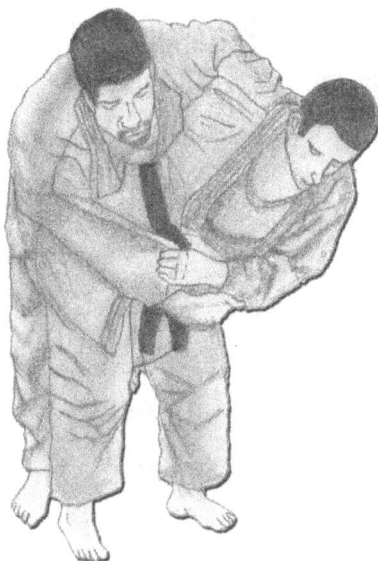

MMA DICTIONARY

UMMAR – Unified Mixed Martial Arts Rules.

UFC – Ultimate Fighting Championship. The first major Mixed Martial Arts competition that involved various differing styles facing each other in an Octagon or eight sided ring. UFC was not the first Mixed Martial Arts promotion, but it was the most exciting as there were little or no rules in the early UFC. The UFC played a huge role in the promotion and legitimization of Mixed Martial Arts. MMA had an unsavory reputation and was viewed as criminal by many authorities. The UFC opened many States in the United States to the notion of MMA as a legitimate Sport and a legitimate business. The UFC was a trailblazer

MMA DICTIONARY

for the popularization of MMA and its success in reaching mass audiences through Pay Per View. The UFC is the largest MMA fight promotion in the United States and has witnessed scores of copycat leagues that were created by competitors in order to reproduce the UFC's success. The UFC created the model that following MMA promoters copied and is a trailblazer in the MMA industry.

MMA DICTIONARY

Uke – Block in the Japanese language. Blocking and defense is more important for K

Underpass – Passing an opponent's guard by going under their leg(s).

Unregulated – Competitions that are not sanctioned by a State or Federal Athletic Commission. Unregulated

MMA DICTIONARY

matches are dangerous and are most likely illegal. In the United States, every State has an Athletic Commission that oversees professional sports, in order to ensure the safety and welfare of the participants.

Upa – Arching the back in defense while a defender is on their back. It can also be used as a BJJ ground grappling reversal technique that results in the defender landing in the guard of the opponent. The defender arches their back and turns towards their shoulder, causing the opponent to turn on to their back.

MMA DICTIONARY

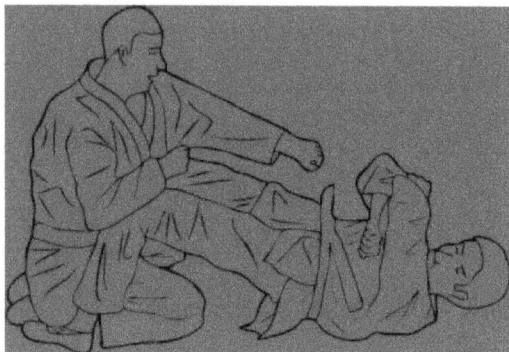

Uppercut – Boxing punching technique that brings the arm up vertically striking the opponent in the chin. It is an effective technique that is delivered from close range. Uppercuts are powerful strikes that frequently result in knockouts.

Ushiro – Reverse or back in the Japanese language.

Ushiro Geri – Back Kick. The Ushiro Geri is an effective Karate technique

MMA DICTIONARY

that generates a large amount of power from the force generated by the hips. Many MMA matches have witnessed a fighter being knocked out or knocked down from a properly placed Ushiro Geri.

V

Vale Tudo – Brazilian MMA competitions that featured little or no rules. It was made famous in the early 1990's and is referenced as an early pioneer of MMA. Techniques, deemed illegal in professional MMA, such as head-butting, were allowed in Vale Tudo matches. Vale Tudo matches are exciting to watch because of their lack of constrictions.

MMA DICTIONARY

Vo Binh Dinh – Vietnamese Martial Art used for repelling foreign invaders.

W

Way – Martial art path undertaken by a student of a specific martial art.

Waza – Technique in the Japanese language.

Weigh In – Fighters have their weight officially registered for regulation purposes before the beginning of a match. This is done publicly to present both fighters and their official weights.

MMA DICTIONARY

White Crane Kung Fu – Chinese
Shaolin derived Kung Fu style that
influenced the creation of Japanese
Karate. Foshan White Crane Kung
Fu was passed on through teachers
and the Bubishi, to Japanese
students who went on to develop
Karate.

MMA DICTIONARY

White, Dana – Famous MMA promoter that expanded and popularized the Ultimate Fighting Championship. He was made popular by his great success in growing the UFC to an international brand name. Dana established licensing deals with various companies to leverage the UFC brand and made MMA a household name. White is a sports celebrity and credited with growing the UFC as well as the sport of MMA.

Wing Chun – Traditional Chinese martial art that is believed to have evolved from the Shaolin Temple. Wing Chun is mostly a striking style, although it incorporates techniques from Chin-na. Wing Chun uses chain punching, fast repetitive punches, as

MMA DICTIONARY

its main fighting technique.

Popularized by Wing Chun
practitioner Bruce Lee who was a
student of Wing Chun Sifu Ip Man.
Although Bruce Lee had
understanding of Wing Chun, he was
never taught the 3rd final form by Ip
Man. Bruce Lee incorporated
techniques from Wing Chun in to his

MMA DICTIONARY

newly created Jeet Kun Do. Wing Chun has been popularized through movies and through mass media. Wing Chun has been unable to compete successfully in Mixed Martial Arts competition with any success.

Worm Guard – BJJ guard used while a defender is on their back. The defender's left leg wraps around the opponent's right leg and the defender's right leg applies pressure to the opponent's waist while the defender grabs the opponent's sleeve to apply push and pull. The Worm Guard is an effective guard for sweeping an opponent.

Wushu – Umbrella name for Chinese martial arts. Wushu is

MMA DICTIONARY

incorrectly named as a style on to itself.

Z

Zanshin – State of awareness in the Japanese language.

Zen – Meditation practiced in China and Japan. Zen practices attempt to achieve stillness of mind and tranquility.

MMA DICTIONARY

Zenkutsu Datchi – Front stance.

Zuffa – Company that purchased the original UFC in 2001. Zuffa is an Italian word that means "brawl" or "fight with no rules".

MMA DICTIONARY

MIKAZUKI PUBLISHING HOUSE™

1) 25 Principles of Martial Arts
2) 25 Principles of Strategy
3) American Antifa
4) American Bookstore Directory
5) Arctic Black Gold
6) Art of War
7) Back to Gold
8) Basketball Team Play Design Book
9) Beginner's Magicians Manual
10) Bernie Sander's Revolution
11) Boxing Coloring Book
12) California's Next Century 2.0
13) Camping Survival Handbook
14) Captain Bligh's Voyage
15) Coming to America Handbook
16) Customer Sales Organizer
17) DIY Comic Book
18) DIY Comic Book Part II
19) Economic Collapse Survival Manual
20) Farrakhan Speaks
21) Fashion Design Shoes Coloring Book
22) Fidel Castro Speaks
23) Find The Ideal Husband
24) Football Play Design Book
25) Freakshow Los Angeles
26) Game Creation Manual

MMA DICTIONARY

27) George Washington's Farewell Address
28) Hagakure
29) History of Aliens
30) Hollywood Talent Agency Directory
31) I Dream in Haiku
32) Internet Connected World
33) Irish Republican Army Manual of Guerrilla Warfare
34) Japan History Coloring Book
35) John Locke's 2nd Treatise on Civil Government
36) Karate 360
37) Karate Fighter Coloring Book
38) Learning Magic
39) Living the Pirate Code
40) Magic as Science and Religion
41) Magicians Coloring Book
42) Make Racists Afraid Again
43) Master Password Organizer Handbook
44) Mikazuki Jujitsu Manual
45) Mikazuki Political Science Manual
46) MMA Coloring Book
47) MMA Dictionary
48) Mythology Coloring Book
49) Mythology Dictionary
50) Native Americana

MMA DICTIONARY

51) Ninja Style
52) Ouija Board Enigma
53) Palloncino
54) Political Advertising Manual
55) Quotes Gone Wild
56) Rappers Rhyme Book
57) Saving America
58) Self-Examination Diary
59) Shinzen Karate
60) Shogun X the Last Immortal
61) Small Arms & Deep Pockets
62) Stories of a Street Performer
63) Storyboard Book
64) Swords & Sails
65) Tao Te Ching
66) The Adventures of Sherlock Holmes
67) The Art of Western Boxing
68) The Book of Five Rings
69) The Bribe Vibe
70) The Card Party
71) The History of Acid Tripping
72) The Man That Made the English Language
73) Tokiwa
74) Triggering Everyone
75) T-Shirt Design Book
76) U.S. Army Anti-Guerrilla Warfare Manual
77) United Nations Charter
78) U.S. Military Boxing Manual

MMA DICTIONARY

If the Mikazuki Publishing House™ book is not available at a bookstore, place a request with the bookstore to order it for you.

Mikazuki Publishing House is a book publisher that specializes in non-fiction. Mikazuki Publishing House believes that Education is the Key to Happiness. Mikazuki Publishing House believes in supporting Independent Bookstores.

MMA DICTIONARY

NOTES

MMA DICTIONARY

NOTES